HOUGHTON MIFFLIN HARCOURT

JOURNEYS

Program Authors

James F. Baumann · David J. Chard · Jamal Cooks
J. David Cooper · Russell Gersten · Marjorie Lipson
Lesley Mandel Morrow · John J. Pikulski · Héctor H. Rivera
Mabel Rivera · Shane Templeton · Sheila W. Valencia
Catherine Valentino · MaryEllen Vogt

Consulting Author
Irene Fountas

HOUGHTON MIFFLIN HARCOURT
School Publishers

ISBN 10:   0-54-725183-1
ISBN 13:   978-0-54-725183-7

5 6 7 8 9 0868 18 17 16 15 14 13 12 11
4500331387

Hello, Reader!

Think about all of the stories you have read. Which one is your favorite so far?

In this book, you will meet characters who help their friends, work hard at school, and solve mysteries. You will even read about a soccer player that you may know. Whatever they do, the characters in these stories always try their best.

Do your best as you read. You will learn even more words!

Sincerely,

The Authors

Three Cheers for Us!

 Big Idea Always try your best.

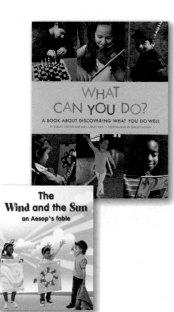

Three Cheers for Us!

Unit 6

Big Idea

Always try
your best.

Paired Selections

Read Together

WORDS TO KNOW

HIGH-FREQUENCY WORDS

teacher

studied

surprised

toward

bear

above

even

pushed

Vocabulary Reader

Context Cards

Words to Know

Read Together

- Read each Context Card.

- Choose two blue words. Use them in sentences.

1

teacher

The art teacher shows how to use a brush.

2

studied

She studied the flower before she drew it.

3 surprised

He was surprised to see such a big statue.

4 toward

He walked slowly toward the art table.

5 bear

The picture of the bear looks very real.

6 above

These shapes hang high above the floor.

7 even

This box has even more crayons in it.

8 pushed

He pushed the clay into new shapes.

Background

Read
Together

✔ **WORDS TO KNOW**   **Art Class**   The art **teacher** pushed the cart of art supplies **toward** the children. They **studied** how to use them. A boy drew a **bear**. A girl drew the sun **above** tall trees. The class **even surprised** their teacher by painting a class picture!

Art Supplies

crayons   **paintbrush**   **watercolors**

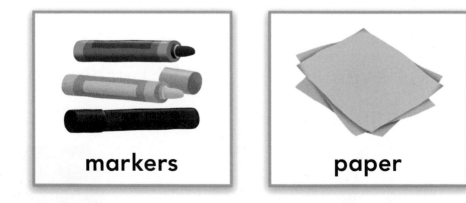

markers   **paper**

Name some other art supplies.

Comprehension

Read Together

✔ **TARGET SKILL**   Compare and Contrast

Remember that when you **compare**, you tell
how things are alike. When you **contrast**,
you tell how things are different. Good
readers compare and contrast things like
characters, settings, or events as they read.
How are markers and a paintbrush alike?
How are they different?

markers   **paintbrush**

As you read **The Dot**, think about how
drawing and painting are the same and
different. Write ideas on a Venn diagram.

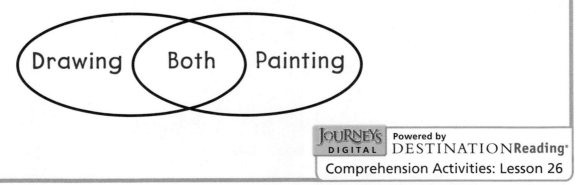

Drawing   Both   Painting

JOURNEYS DIGITAL   Powered by DESTINATIONReading
Comprehension Activities: Lesson 26

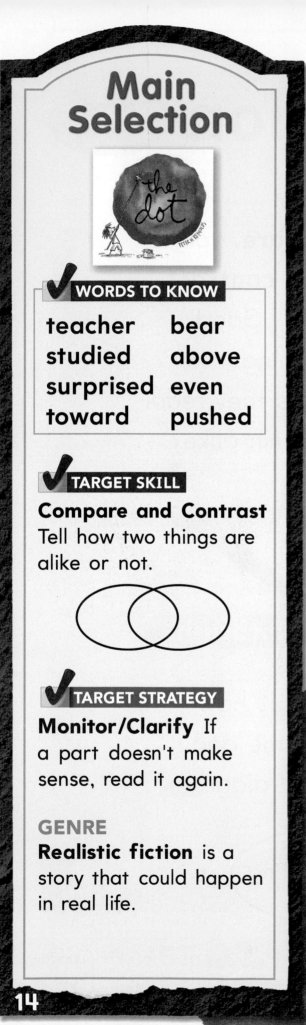

WORDS TO KNOW

teacher	bear
studied	above
surprised	even
toward	pushed

TARGET SKILL

Compare and Contrast
Tell how two things are alike or not.

TARGET STRATEGY

Monitor/Clarify If a part doesn't make sense, read it again.

GENRE

Realistic fiction is a story that could happen in real life.

14

Meet the Author and Illustrator

Peter H. Reynolds

It took Peter H. Reynolds a year and a half to write **The Dot.** He named his character Vashti after a young girl he met at a coffee shop. Mr. Reynolds wrote **Ish** as a follow-up book to **The Dot**.

the dot

by Peter H. Reynolds

Essential Question

How are ways to make art the same and different?

15

Art class was over, but Vashti sat
glued to her chair.

Her paper was empty.

Vashti's teacher leaned over the blank paper.
"Ah! A polar bear in a snow storm," she said.
"Very funny!" said Vashti. "I just CAN'T draw!"

Her teacher smiled.

"Just make a mark and
see where it takes you."

Vashti grabbed a marker and
gave the paper a good, strong jab.

"There!"

Her teacher picked up the paper
and studied it carefully.

"Hmmmmm."

She pushed the paper toward
Vashti and quietly said,
"Now sign it."

Vashti thought for a moment.

"Well, maybe I can't draw,
but I CAN sign my name."

The next week,
when Vashti walked into art class,
she was surprised to see what was
hanging above her teacher's desk.

It was the little dot
she had drawn—HER DOT!
All framed in swirly gold!

✔ **STOP AND THINK**
Compare and Contrast
Does Vashti have a different
feeling about her dot now?
Explain.

"Hmmph!
I can make a better dot than THAT!"

She opened her
never-before-used set of
watercolors and set to work.

Vashti painted and painted.
A red dot. A purple dot.
A yellow dot. A blue dot.

The blue mixed with the yellow.
She discovered that she could make
a GREEN dot.

Vashti kept experimenting.
Lots of little dots in many colors.

"If I can make little dots,
I can make BIG dots, too."

Vashti splashed her colors with
a bigger brush on bigger paper
to make bigger dots.

Vashti even made a dot
by NOT painting a dot.

At the school art show a few weeks later,
Vashti's many dots made quite a splash.

Vashti noticed a little boy gazing up at her.

"You're a really great artist.
I wish I could draw," he said.

"I bet you can," said Vashti.

"ME? No, not me. I can't draw
a straight line with a ruler."

Vashti smiled.

She handed the boy
a blank sheet of paper.
"Show me."

The boy's pencil shook
as he drew his line.

Vashti stared at the boy's squiggle.
And then she said . . .

"Sign it."

Your Turn

Be an Artist

Create Dot Art Create your own artwork from dots. Use one dot or many dots. Share your artwork with a partner. Tell how your artworks are alike and different. PARTNERS

Turn and Talk — Compare Artworks

Look through **The Dot** again with a partner. Choose two of Vashti's artworks. Talk about how they are alike and how they are different.

COMPARE AND CONTRAST

Connect to Social Studies

✔ **WORDS TO KNOW**

teacher	bear
studied	above
surprised	even
toward	pushed

GENRE

A **biography** tells about events in a person's life. Find facts about artists' lives in this article.

TEXT FOCUS

Captions tell more information about a photo or picture. Use the captions and photos to find out more about pieces of art.

Artists Create Art!

by Anne Rogers

An artist makes art. Some artists paint pictures. Other artists make things.

David Wynne made this grizzly bear. It stands above a pond in New York.

David Wynne's sculpture "Grizzly Bear" is at the Donald M. Kendall Sculpture Gardens.

Seated Figures, Study for "A Sunday Afternoon on the Island of the Grande Jatte" by Georges Seurat

Georges Seurat went to art school in France. Look at his painting. Once you have studied it, you will see it is made of many brushstrokes. Are you surprised?

Tressa "Grandma" Prisbrey used glass bottles to make her art. She learned by herself. No teacher helped her.

Grandma Prisbrey made the wishing well shown below. She even made a building where her grandchildren played.

wishing well

Now turn toward a window. Think about what would happen if you pushed your paintbrush across the sky. What would your picture be?

Making Connections

📖 Text to Self

Talk About Feelings How do you feel when you try your best? Compare and share ideas with a partner.

📖 Text to Text

Connect to Art How are the artworks in the selections alike? Which artist do you think Vashti would like? Tell why.

🌐 Text to World

Make a List Make a list of ways that an artist can use his or her artwork.

Grammar

Exclamations A sentence that shows a strong feeling is called an **exclamation**. An exclamation begins with a capital letter and ends with an exclamation point.

You are a great artist!

That is such a beautiful painting!

Art class is so much fun!

Try This!

Write each exclamation correctly.
Use another sheet of paper.

1. i can't wait for our school art show

2. this will be the best show ever

3. we are going to have a great time

4. ramon made such a tiny drawing

5. it is my very favorite in the show

Grammar in Writing

When you revise your writing, try using some exclamations.

Write to Respond

 **Voice**   When you write **opinion sentences**, you can help readers hear your voice. Use exclamations to show your strong feelings.

Jill wrote an opinion about Vashti. Then she changed a sentence to an exclamation.

Revised Draft

really great   !
I think Vashti is a ~~good~~ artist.

Writing Traits Checklist

 Voice   Did I use exclamations to show my strong feelings?

 Are there any sentences that do not help explain my opinion? Did I delete them?

✔ Did I use the correct end marks?

In Jill's Final Copy, how does she show that she feels strongly about her opinion? Now edit your writing. Use the Checklist.

Final Copy

A Great Artist

I think Vashti is a really great artist!

One reason is she thinks of lots of ways to paint dots.

Another reason is that her paintings are very colorful.

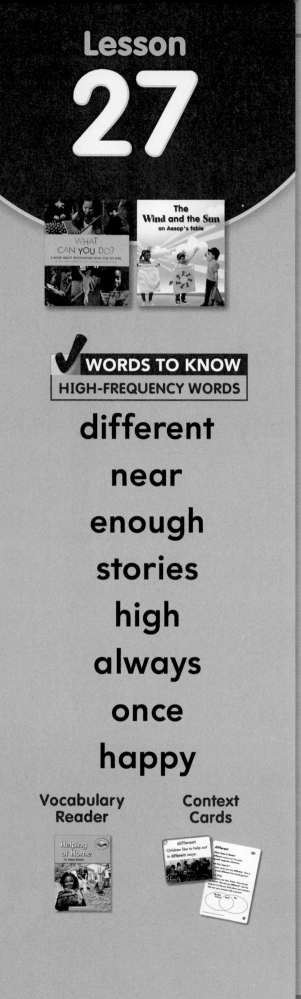

different

near

enough

stories

high

always

once

happy

Vocabulary
Reader

Context
Cards

Words to Know

- Read each Context Card.

- Make up a new sentence that uses a blue word.

1

different

Children like to help out in different ways.

2

near

The girl helps plant flowers near the porch.

3 enough

Is there **enough** paint for everyone?

4 stories

They read silly **stories** to each other.

5 high

The girl helped him swing **high!**

6 always

She **always** helps her brother tie his shoes.

7 once

The boys cleaned up **once** they were done.

8 happy

She was **happy** to help wash the dog.

Background

✓ **WORDS TO KNOW** **Having Fun** What are some different ways to have fun? You can ride a bike near your home. You can swing high in the air. You can make up funny stories. Always take enough time to learn and have fun! Once you do, you will feel happy.

Ways to Have Fun

Read a book.

Ride a bike.

Swing high.

Kick a ball.

Tap a drum.

Name some ways you have fun.

Comprehension

✔ **TARGET SKILL** Text and Graphic Features

When authors write about real things, they may use special text and features. **Special text** can be titles, labels, or captions. **Features** can be photos, graphs, maps, or drawings. Good readers use special text and features to get more information.

Graph   Map   Drawing

As you read **What Can You Do?**, notice the text and photos. Tell why they are used.

Feature	Purpose

JOURNEYS DIGITAL **Powered by** DESTINATIONReading®
Comprehension Activities: Lesson 27

45

✓ **WORDS TO KNOW**

different	high
near	always
enough	once
stories	happy

✓ **TARGET SKILL**

Text and Graphic Features Tell how words go with photos.

✓ **TARGET STRATEGY**

Analyze/Evaluate Tell how you feel about the text, and why.

GENRE

Informational text gives facts about a topic.

Meet the Author and Photographer

Shelley Rotner

Shelley Rotner is both an author and an award-winning photographer. She has taken photographs of children from around the world.

Meet the Author

Sheila M. Kelly

What a team! Together, Sheila M. Kelly and Shelley Rotner have written about moms, dads, and grandparents. In this book, the two authors show that everyone has talents.

WHAT CAN YOU DO?

A BOOK ABOUT DISCOVERING WHAT YOU DO WELL

BY SHELLEY ROTNER AND SHEILA KELLY, ED.D.

PHOTOGRAPHS BY SHELLEY ROTNER

Essential Question

How do words and photos together give information?

47

"I know a boy
who can draw very
well and a girl who can
climb very high."

"We are all good at doing something.
We're always learning new things
as we get older."

"I like to swim
and learned how to float.
I had to practice.
Once I learned, I
felt like I could float for hours!"

"My little brother
is better on skis.
He can ski much faster
than I can."

We're happy when we
do something well,
whatever that might be.

"Reading is easy for me,
but math is much harder.
I'd like to be better at math, though."

STOP AND THINK
Text and Graphic Features
Why does the author show
these two pictures together?

"I can't read very well yet.
I wish I could."

It can take a long time
to be good at something.
If we practice, things get
easier and easier to do.

Marie knows how to spell, and Jill prints well. Gene is really good at anything that has to do with computers.

"I haven't
discovered what
I'm good at yet."

Nathan writes funny stories about science.
Some of the funniest ones are
about a baby robot!
Beth likes to build.
The biggest tower she ever built
was taller than she is!

"I made the soccer team this year.
I hope I play well enough to score a goal."
"I see lots of things in the park.
I look near and far.
Things look much closer
through my binoculars!"

We all like to do what we do best.
When things are hard,
we need help to learn.
We might say, "I don't get it."

We're good at different things.

"I feed the baby myself now. When she gets bigger, she will not need help."

"I can fix my brother's wagon. I'm younger than my brother, but I'm good at fixing things."

"I got my training wheels off earlier than I thought I would.
I felt very proud!"

"The kids made me captain of our team. That was one of the happiest days of my life."

We have schoolwork, acting, singing,
dancing, playing games, or sports!
We all have something we do well.

What can you do?

Your Turn

What I Can Do!

Write About You Write about a time you learned to do something new. Tell what you learned and how you learned it. How did you feel when you knew you could do it? Draw a picture to go with your story.   PERSONAL RESPONSE

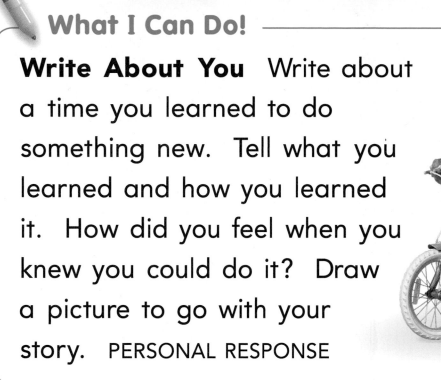

Turn and Talk — Who's Talking?

Look at page 59 with a partner. What do the quotation marks tell you about the words on this page? Talk about how the photos help you understand the words.

TEXT AND GRAPHIC FEATURES

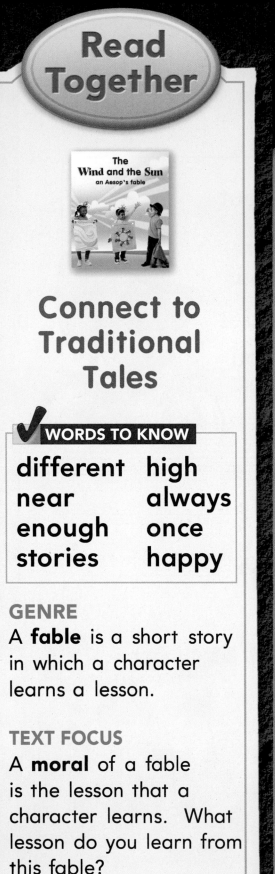

Connect to Traditional Tales

✔ **WORDS TO KNOW**

different	high
near	always
enough	once
stories	happy

GENRE

A **fable** is a short story in which a character learns a lesson.

TEXT FOCUS

A **moral** of a fable is the lesson that a character learns. What lesson do you learn from this fable?

Readers' Theater

The Wind and the Sun

an Aesop's fable

Cast

📖 Narrator

🌀 Wind

☀ Sun

🎩 Traveler

📖 **Narrator** Sometimes stories teach a lesson. In this story, Wind and Sun have different ideas about who is stronger.

🌀 **Wind** I am stronger.

Sun No, I am stronger.

Wind That's enough bragging. Let's have a contest. I know **I** will win.

Sun I'll be happy to have a contest.

Wind Okay. I see a traveler coming near. Whoever gets the traveler to take off that coat is stronger.

Narrator First Wind began to blow very hard. Once Wind started, it did not stop.

Traveler That wind is always so cold. I need to wrap my coat tight around me.

Narrator Then Sun began to shine from **high** up in the sky. It was shining gently. The air got warmer and warmer.

Traveler Now it's nice and warm. I can take off my heavy coat.

Narrator The moral is: "It is better to use kindness instead of force."

Making Connections

Read Together

Text to Self

Write About Yourself
Write sentences that tell what you do best.

Text to Text

Talk About It In a group, decide what Wind and Sun should do if they want the traveler to put his coat back on.

Text to World

Connect to Social Studies Think of a person you know who tries hard. Write about how that person does his or her best.

Grammar

Read Together

Kinds of Sentences Different kinds of sentences have different jobs. Every sentence begins with a capital letter and ends with an end mark.

A **statement** tells something. **S**he is in a play**.**

A **question** asks something. **W**ould you like to be in plays**?**

An **exclamation** shows a strong feeling. **I** love acting in plays**!**

Write each sentence correctly.
Use another sheet of paper.

1. Emma can climb high

2. did Jamal learn to ski

3. She is a great dancer?

4. my friend builds things

5. What can you do.

Grammar in Writing

When you revise your writing, try using some different kinds of sentences.

Write to Respond

✓ Sentence Fluency Good **opinion sentences** give reasons. Sometimes you can explain a reason by using the word **because**.

Raul wrote an opinion about skiing. Then he added words to explain his first reason.

Revised Draft

because you can go fast
It is exciting.
‸

Writing Traits Checklist

✓ Sentence Fluency Did I use the word **because** to explain one reason?

✓ Does my topic sentence tell my opinion?

✓ Do my sentences end with the correct mark?

✓ Did I check my spelling with a dictionary?

What words does Raul use to explain why skiing is exciting? Use the Checklist to revise your sentences.

Fun on Skis

Skiing is so much fun!

It is exciting because you can go fast.

I also like jumping over big piles of snow.

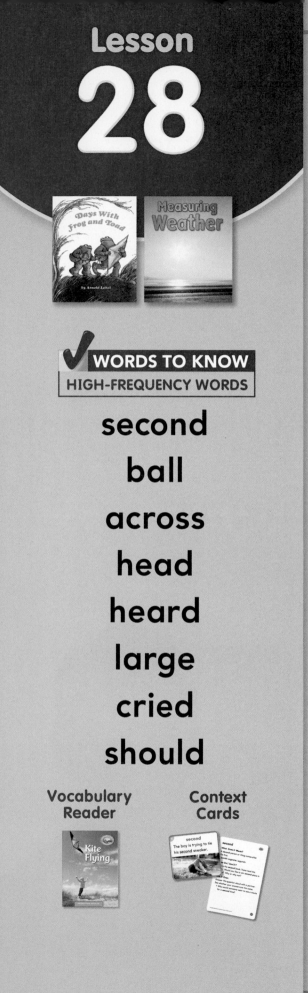

Days With Frog and Toad
by Arnold Lobel

Measuring Weather

✓ WORDS TO KNOW
HIGH-FREQUENCY WORDS

second

ball

across

head

heard

large

cried

should

Vocabulary Reader

Context Cards

Kite Flying

Words to Know

- Read each Context Card.

- Ask a question that uses one of the blue words.

1 second

The boy is trying to tie his second sneaker.

2 ball

She practiced until she could hit the ball well.

3. across

The runners dashed across the finish line.

4. head

He hit the ball with his head to make a goal.

5. heard

The children heard clapping at the end.

6. large

It was not too hard to ride up the large hill.

7. cried

"We can do it!" cried the team.

8. should

The teacher said that she should try again.

Background

✓ WORDS TO KNOW **Flying a Kite** Have you heard that flying a kite is fun? You should try it on a breezy day. Get a kite and a large ball of string. Hold the kite above your head. Run across the grass. If that doesn't work, try a second time. Soon you will have cried, "The kite is flying!"

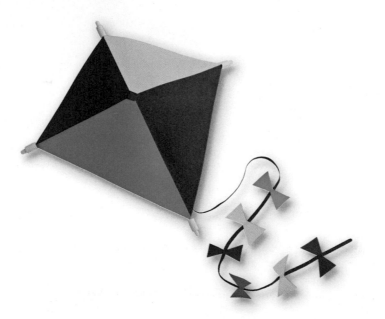

- What does cried mean in the sentence?
- Did you ever fly a kite? Tell about it.
- Would you like to fly one? Why or why not?

Comprehension

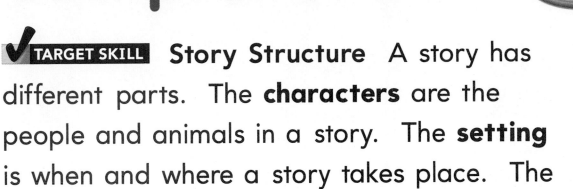

✓ **TARGET SKILL** **Story Structure** A story has different parts. The **characters** are the people and animals in a story. The **setting** is when and where a story takes place. The **plot** is the order of story events. The plot tells about a problem the characters have and what they do to solve it.

What problem does this character have?

As you read **The Kite**, think about Frog and Toad's problem and how it is solved.

Characters	Setting
Plot	

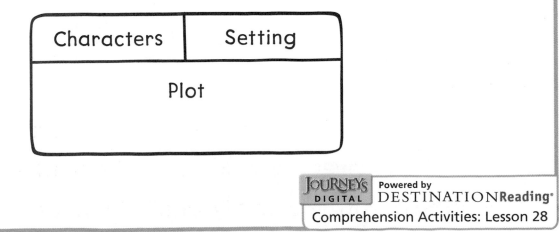

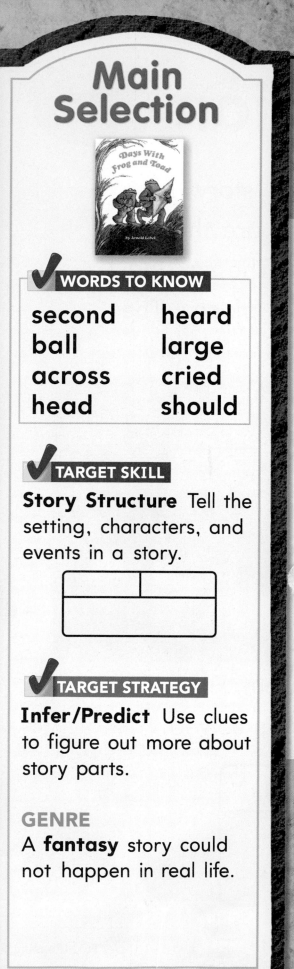

✔ **WORDS TO KNOW**

second	heard
ball	large
across	cried
head	should

✔ **TARGET SKILL**

Story Structure Tell the setting, characters, and events in a story.

✔ **TARGET STRATEGY**

Infer/Predict Use clues to figure out more about story parts.

GENRE

A **fantasy** story could not happen in real life.

Meet the Author and Illustrator

Arnold Lobel

Arnold Lobel drew many animals before he came up with the frog and toad characters. During vacations with his family in Vermont, Mr. Lobel watched children play with frogs and toads. Soon the animals were starring in his books.

The Kite

from Days with Frog and Toad

by Arnold Lobel

The Kite

Frog and Toad went out
to fly a kite.
They went to a large meadow
where the wind was strong.
"Our kite will fly up and up,"
said Frog.
"It will fly all the way up
to the top of the sky."
"Toad," said Frog,
"I will hold the ball of string.
You hold the kite and run."

Toad ran across the meadow.
He ran as fast as his short legs
could carry him.
The kite went up in the air.
It fell to the ground with a bump.
Toad heard laughter.
Three robins were sitting in a bush.

"That kite will not fly,"
said the robins.
"You may as well give up."

Toad ran back to Frog.
"Frog," said Toad,
"this kite will not fly. I give up."

✔ **STOP AND THINK**
Story Structure What problem
do Frog and Toad have?

"We must make a second try," said
Frog. "Wave the kite over your head.
Perhaps that will make it fly."

Toad ran back across the meadow.
He waved the kite over his head.

The kite went up in the air
and then fell down with a thud.
"What a joke!" said the robins.
"That kite will never
get off the ground."

Toad ran back to Frog.

"This kite is a joke," he said.

"It will never get off the ground."

"We have to make

a third try," said Frog.

"Wave the kite over your head

and jump up and down.

Perhaps that will make it fly."

Toad ran across the meadow again.
He waved the kite over his head.
He jumped up and down.
The kite went up in the air and
crashed down into the grass.

"That kite is junk," said the robins.
"Throw it away and go home."
Toad ran back to Frog.
"This kite is junk," he said.
"I think we should throw
it away and go home."

"Toad," said Frog,
"we need one more try.
Wave the kite over your head.
Jump up and down
and shout UP KITE UP."

Toad ran across the meadow.
He waved the kite over his head.
He jumped up and down.
He shouted, "UP KITE UP!"

The kite flew into the air.
It climbed higher and higher.
"We did it!" cried Toad.

"Yes," said Frog.
"If a running try
did not work,
a running and waving try
did not work,
and a running, waving,
and jumping try
did not work,
I knew that
a running, waving, jumping,
and shouting try
just had to work."

The robins flew out of the bush.
But they could not fly
as high as the kite.
Frog and Toad sat
and watched their kite.
It seemed to be flying
way up at the top of the sky.

Your Turn

What Next?

Change the Ending How do the robins make Toad feel when his kite will not fly? What do you think the robins should say the next time they see Toad? Act out a new story ending with a partner. Take turns being Toad and the robins.
PARTNERS

 **Compare Characters**

Talk with a partner about how Frog and Toad are alike and different. Explain how Frog helps Toad solve the kite problem. STORY STRUCTURE

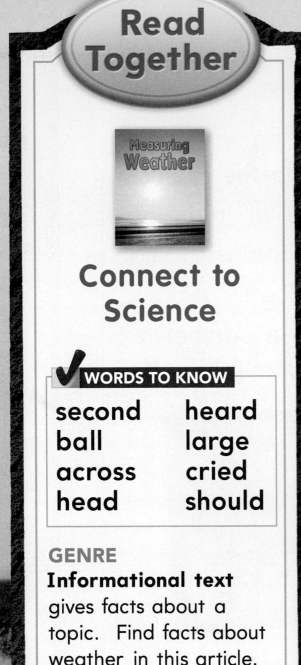

Connect to Science

✓ **WORDS TO KNOW**

second	heard
ball	large
across	cried
head	should

GENRE
Informational text gives facts about a topic. Find facts about weather in this article.

TEXT FOCUS
A **graph** is a drawing that uses numbers, pictures, or symbols to give information. What does the graph on p. 96 show?

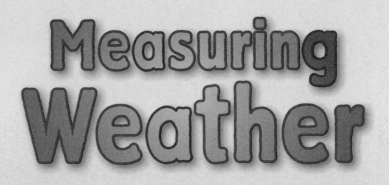

Measuring Weather

There are different tools for measuring weather.

Have you ever heard of a windsock? It shows which way the wind blows.

A rain gauge measures how much rain falls. A large storm will bring a lot of rain.

A thermometer measures temperature. Temperature is how warm or cool something is.

On a hot day, your friends might have cried, "Let's ride bikes and play ball!"

On a cold day, your mother might have said, "You should wear a hat on your head."

When you know the temperature, you know what to wear.

Look at the bars across the graph.
Each bar shows the temperature for a day.
Which day was the hottest? Which day
was the coolest? What was the temperature
on the second day of the week?

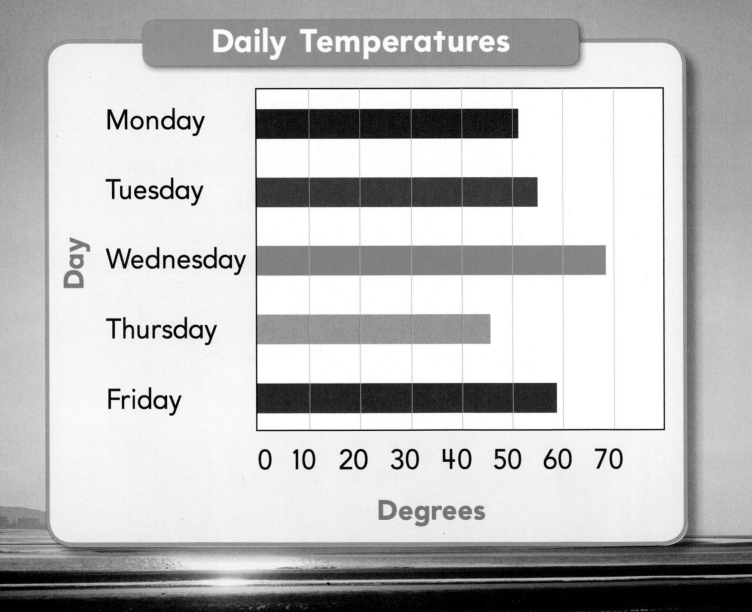

Daily Temperatures

Day

Monday
Tuesday
Wednesday
Thursday
Friday

0 10 20 30 40 50 60 70

Degrees

Making Connections

Read Together

Text to Self

Think and Share Think about the fun Frog and Toad had on the windy day. Tell a partner what you do on windy days.

Text to Text

Write to Describe What was the weather like when Frog and Toad flew a kite? Write about it. Use words that tell how things looked, moved, and sounded.

Text to World

Connect to Social Studies Draw a picture that shows the different kinds of weather in your state.

Grammar

Read Together

Kinds of Adjectives Some adjectives describe by telling how things **taste, smell, sound,** or **feel.**

Taste	We ate **sweet** berries before we flew kites.
Smell	The air smelled **fresh** and **clean**.
Sound	We gave a **loud** cheer when our kites flew up!
Feel	The **warm** sun shined down on us.

Work with a partner. Find the adjective in each sentence. Decide if it tells how something tastes, smells, sounds, or feels. Then use the adjective in a new sentence.

1. Sam shared his sour pickles at our picnic.

2. Our kites flew in the cool breeze.

3. Some crickets made noisy chirps.

4. We ate some salty chips.

5. Our pie smelled delicious!

Grammar in Writing

When you revise your writing, look for places to add adjectives to tell how things taste, smell, sound, or feel.

Write to Respond

✔ **Word Choice** When you write **opinion sentences**, don't use the same words again and again. Use different words to tell more. Matt wrote about the robins. Later, he changed words to make his ideas clearer.

Revised Draft

The three robins were mean.
laughed at Frog and Toad.
They ~~did mean things.~~
^

 Writing Traits Checklist

 Word Choice Did I add adjectives and other exact words to make my ideas clear?

✔ Did I write reasons that explain my opinion?

✔ Did I use a dictionary, Glossary, or word list to check my spelling?

Which words in Matt's final copy explain how the robins were mean? Now revise your writing. Use the Checklist.

Final Copy

The Mean Robins

The three robins were mean.

They laughed at Frog and Toad.

The noisy, rude robins

said that Frog and

Toad's kite was junk.

✓ **WORDS TO KNOW**
HIGH-FREQUENCY WORDS

leaves

any

happened

gone

hello

behind

idea

almost

Vocabulary
Reader

Context
Cards

Words to Know

Read Together

- Read each Context Card.
- Describe a picture, using the blue word.

1

leaves

The ladybugs are on the leaves of this plant.

2

any

There aren't any bugs in the spider web.

3 happened
What happened to the wasps' nest?

4 gone
The moths are gone, but they left eggs.

5 hello
The bees seem to say hello to each other.

6 behind
Do you see the grass behind the ant hill?

7 idea
Here is an idea, or plan, for a project.

8 almost
This bug has almost finished eating.

Background

Read Together

✔ **WORDS TO KNOW** **How Insects Move**

To learn how insects move, here's an idea. Say hello loudly. Almost any insect will move. An ant will crawl away. A ladybug will fly from the leaves. A grasshopper will hop fast behind tall grass. Write about what happened before the insects are gone.

Insects

grasshopper

ant

ladybug

bumblebee

What does leaves mean in the sentence?
Name some more insects.

Comprehension

Read
Together

✔ **TARGET SKILL** Cause and Effect

Remember that one story event can lead
to another. The **cause** is the reason why
something happens. The **effect**
is what happens. Good readers
think about cause and effect to
better understand what happens
in a story and why it happens.

Cause: The boy played ball inside.
What is the **effect**?

As you read **A Boat Disappears**, think
about what Skeet does to find his boat.

What happens?	Why?

JOURNEYS
DIGITAL Powered by
DESTINATIONReading®
Comprehension Activities: Lesson 29

Main Selection

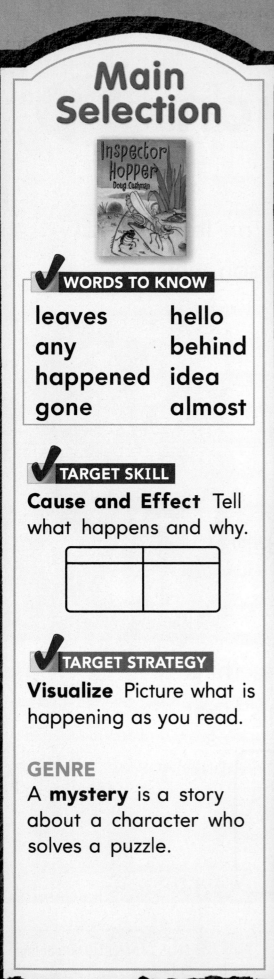

Inspector Hopper
Doug Cushman

✓ **WORDS TO KNOW**

leaves	hello
any	behind
happened	idea
gone	almost

✓ **TARGET SKILL**
Cause and Effect Tell what happens and why.

✓ **TARGET STRATEGY**
Visualize Picture what is happening as you read.

GENRE
A **mystery** is a story about a character who solves a puzzle.

106

Meet the Author and Illustrator
Doug Cushman

Doug Cushman says, "A good character will almost write a book by himself." Some of his characters include Aunt Eater, a mystery-solving anteater, and Nick Trunk, an elephant detective. In this story, you will meet Inspector Hopper and McBugg.

A Boat Disappears

from Inspector Hopper

by Doug Cushman

Essential Question

How do some story events make other events happen?

Solving a mystery can be tricky. You may
look behind and beneath things for clues.
You are almost sure to solve it if
you go to a helpful detective,
like the one in this story.

A Boat
Disappears

Skeet walked into the office
of Inspector Hopper.
"My boat disappeared," he said.
"That *is* a mystery,"
said Inspector Hopper.
"Tell us what happened."

"I sailed my boat this morning,"
said Skeet.
"Then I went to lunch.
When I came back after lunch,
my boat was gone!"

"What did your boat look like?"
asked Inspector Hopper.
"Here is a picture," said Skeet.
"It looks like a leaf," said McBugg.
"It *is* a leaf," said Skeet,
"but it is a good boat."

"We will take your case,"
said Inspector Hopper.
"Show us where your boat was
the last time you saw it.
Let's go, McBugg!"

✔️ **STOP AND THINK**
Cause and Effect
Why did Skeet go to
see Inspector Hopper?

They all went to the lake.
"Here is where my boat was,"
said Skeet.

"Hmm," said Inspector Hopper.
"I don't see any footprints.
But wait! What is this?"

"It looks like a piece of my boat,"
said Skeet.

"Here is another piece,"
said Inspector Hopper.

"Let's follow this trail."

They followed the trail of boat pieces.

The trail went past a water spout.

"Hello, Eensy Weensy,"

said Inspector Hopper.

"We are looking for a missing boat."

"What does it look like?"

asked Eensy Weensy.

"Here is a picture," said Skeet.

"It looks like a leaf,"

said Eensy Weensy.

"It *is* a leaf," said Skeet,

"but it is a good boat."

"I have not seen your boat,"
said Eensy Weensy.
"I'm trying to get back up
this water spout.
The rain washed me out."
"Thank you anyway,"
said Inspector Hopper.

Inspector Hopper, McBugg, and Skeet
followed the trail.
"Hello, Sally," said Inspector Hopper.
"We are looking for a missing boat.
Here is a picture of it."
"It looks like a leaf," said Sally.
"It *is* a leaf," said Skeet,
"but it is a good boat."

"I have not seen it," said Sally.
"I have been jogging all morning.
I have already jogged three feet."
"Thank you anyway,"
said Inspector Hopper.
Inspector Hopper, McBugg, and Skeet
followed the trail.

"Hello, Conrad," said Inspector Hopper.
"We are looking for a missing boat.
Here is a picture of it."
"I have seen it," said Conrad.
"Hooray!" said Skeet.
"Where is it?"

"I ate it," said Conrad.

"What?" said Skeet.

"You ate my boat?"

"Yes," said Conrad.

"It looked like a leaf.

So I ate it.

I did not know it was your boat."

"What will I do now?" asked Skeet.

Inspector Hopper looked around.
"There are many leaves here,"
he said.
"Perhaps Conrad can help you pick
out a new boat."
"I would be happy to help,"
said Conrad.
"Thank you," said Skeet.
"Maybe you can pick out a boat
that isn't so yummy."
"That is a good idea," said Conrad.

"Another mystery solved!"
said Inspector Hopper.
"I wonder what a boat tastes like?"
asked McBugg."
"Let's go home,"
said Inspector Hopper.

You're the Detective

Write a Mystery Think about a time when you lost something. What happened? What clues did you use to find it? Write a story to tell how you solved the mystery.

PERSONAL RESPONSE

Turn and Talk — A Mystery Solved

What happened when Conrad saw Skeet's boat? Why did this happen? Talk about it with a partner. Then tell what happened next in the story. CAUSE AND EFFECT

Connect to Poetry

✔ **WORDS TO KNOW**

leaves	hello
any	behind
happened	idea
gone	almost

GENRE

Poetry uses the sound of words to show pictures and feelings. Which rhyming words make the poems fun to hear and say?

TEXT FOCUS

Rhythm is a pattern of beats, like music. Clap along with the rhythm of the poems.

Busy Bugs

How do you think this poet got the idea to write a snail poem? Read how the snail says hello to the Sun.

Caracol, caracol

Caracol, caracol,

saca tus cuernos al sol.

To a Snail

Poke your head out, little one.

Time to say, "Good morning, Sun!"

traditional Spanish rhyme

Look for bugs behind rocks, on leaves, or in the grass. If a bug has wings, it may be gone before you know what happened.

Song of the Bugs

Some bugs pinch
And some bugs creep
Some bugs buzz themselves to sleep
Buzz Buzz Buzz Buzz
This is the song of the bugs.

Some bugs fly
When the moon is high
Some bugs make a light in the sky
Flicker, flicker firefly
This is the song of the bugs.

by Margaret Wise Brown

On almost any rainy day you will be sure to see worms. Watch them move!

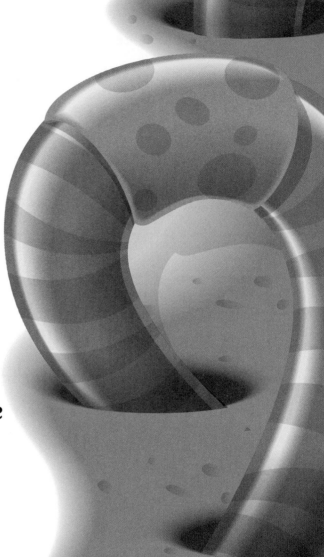

Worm

Squiggly
Wiggly
Wriggly
Jiggly
Ziggly
Higgly
Piggly
Worm.

Watch it wiggle
Watch it wriggle
See it squiggle
See it squirm!

by Mary Ann Hoberman

Write About Bugs

Choose a bug you know about. Write a poem about it. Use rhyming words. Use words to tell what the bug looks like and how it moves.

Making Connections

Text to Self

Write a Caption Draw a picture of your favorite bug. Write a caption that tells how it moves.

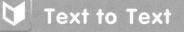

Text to Text

Connect to Music Make up a bug song that Inspector Hopper might sing.

Text to World

Discuss Bugs Tell what kinds of bugs are in your state. List books and other things to help you find out more about those bugs.

Grammar

Read Together

Adverbs Adverbs are words that describe verbs. They can tell **how, where, when,** or **how much** something is. Many, but not all, adverbs end with -ly.

Adverbs	
How	The boat moves **quickly** in the water. They **carefully** steered the boat.
Where	They're **here**! The water splashed **everywhere**.
When	The bugs woke up **early** in the morning. They went to bed **late**.
How much	They kicked a ball **very** hard. The ball flew by **too** fast.

Work with a partner. Read each sentence and find the adverb. Decide if it tells how, where, when, or how much. Then say a new sentence, using the adverb.

1. Ned slowly unpacked the picnic basket.

2. His friends walk to get there.

3. Fred was very tired from the trip.

4. Bea cheerfully told a joke.

5. They want to have picnics often.

Grammar in Writing

When you revise your writing, look for places where you can add adverbs.

Write to Respond

 Ideas   Before writing an **opinion paragraph**, list your opinion and reasons for that opinion. Think of examples to explain your reasons.

Tara wanted to write about Inspector Hopper. To help find good reasons and examples, she looked through the story again.

Explore a Topic

Prewrite Checklist

 Did I list my opinion?

☑ Did I give a few good reasons?

☑ Do my examples explain my reasons?

Read Tara's plan. What is her opinion? What are her reasons? Plan your opinion paragraph. Use the Checklist. Then write your draft.

Planning Chart

My Opinion

Inspector Hopper = good detective

First Reason

gets facts

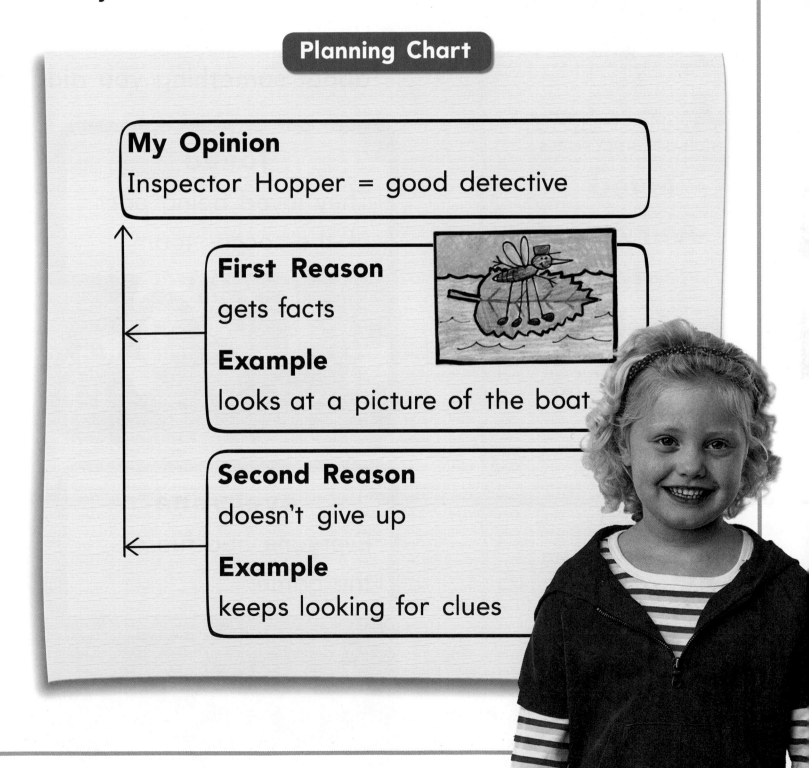

Example

looks at a picture of the boat

Second Reason

doesn't give up

Example

keeps looking for clues

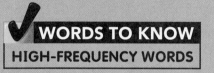

✓ **WORDS TO KNOW**
HIGH-FREQUENCY WORDS

loved

everyone

brothers

field

sorry

only

people

most

Vocabulary
Reader

Context
Cards

Words to Know

Read Together

- Read each Context Card.

- Use a blue word to tell about something you did.

1

loved

They loved being part of the soccer team.

2

everyone

Everyone had fun at the game.

3 brothers
The brothers are on the same team.

4 field
The field was wet after the rain.

5 sorry
The girl was sorry she couldn't play today.

6 only
The Reds are ahead by only one point.

7 people
People were happy after the game.

8 most
The team cheered most for their coach.

Background Read Together

✔ **WORDS TO KNOW**   **Mia Hamm**   Mia Hamm has never been sorry to be playing sports. Even when she was little, she loved soccer the most. She learned from her brothers and sisters. At only fifteen, Mia played on the United States soccer team. Many people watched Mia on the field. Everyone cheered!

Have you ever won anything?
What did it feel like to win?

Comprehension

✓ **TARGET SKILL** **Understanding Characters**

Remember that **characters** are the people and animals in a story. You can learn about story characters from the things they say and do. Good readers use these clues to figure out how characters feel and why they do the things they do.

How do these characters feel? What clues helped you?

As you read **Winners Never Quit!**, think about what Mia says and how she acts.

Speaking	Acting	Feeling

Main Selection

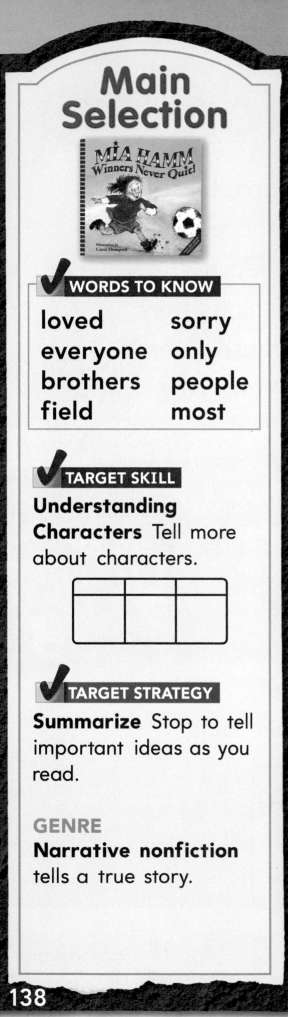

MIA HAMM
Winners Never Quit!
Illustrations by
Carol Thompson

✔ **WORDS TO KNOW**

loved	sorry
everyone	only
brothers	people
field	most

✔ **TARGET SKILL**

Understanding Characters Tell more about characters.

✔ **TARGET STRATEGY**

Summarize Stop to tell important ideas as you read.

GENRE
Narrative nonfiction tells a true story.

Meet the Author

Mia Hamm

Mia Hamm went from playing football to soccer at age fourteen. She became one of the best women's soccer players ever. She knows what it takes to be a good teammate!

Meet the Illustrator

Carol Thompson

Carol Thompson has won many awards for illustrating children's picture books. She also makes greeting cards. She lives in England with her family.

Winners Never Quit!

by Mia Hamm

illustrated by Carol Thompson

Essential Question

What can you learn from story characters?

139

Mia loved basketball.

Mia loved baseball.

But most of all, Mia loved
soccer. She played every
day with her brothers
and sisters.

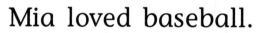

Tap, tap, tap. Her toes kept the ball right
where she wanted it. Then, *smack*! She'd
kick the ball straight into the net. **Goal!**
Everyone on her team would cheer.

But sometimes it didn't work that way.
One day, no matter how hard she tried,
Mia couldn't score a goal.

The ball sailed to
the left of the net.

Or to the right.

Or her sister Lovdy,
the goalie, saved the
ball with her hands.

No goal.

No cheering.

"Too bad, Mia,"
her brother Garrett
said. "Better luck
next time!"

But Mia didn't want
better luck next time.
She wanted better
luck *now*.

"I Quit!"

Mia said.

"You can't quit!" Lovdy said. Then we'll only have two people on our team."

"Come on, Mia," her sister Caroline pleaded. "You always quit when you start losing."

"Just keep playing, Mia," Garrett said. "It'll be fun."

But losing wasn't fun. Mia stomped
back to the house.

✔️ **STOP AND THINK**
Understanding Characters
Why would Mia rather quit
than lose?

"Quitter!"

"Quitter!" Lovdy yelled.
Mia didn't care.
She'd rather quit than lose.

The next day, Mia ran outside, ready to play soccer. When she got there, the game had already started.

"Hey!" she yelled. "Why didn't you wait for me?"

Garrett stopped playing.

"Sorry, Mia," he said. "But quitters can't play on my team."

"Yeah," said Lovdy. "If you can't learn to lose, you can't play."

Garrett passed the ball to
Tiffany. Martin ran to steal it.
Tiffany dashed around him
and took a shot at the goal.
Lovdy blocked it.

Mia just stood
by the side and
watched.

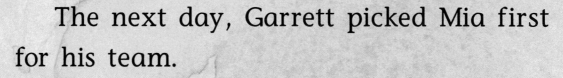

The next day, Garrett picked Mia first for his team.

Mia got the ball. She dribbled down the field. *Smack!* She kicked the ball toward the goal.

And Lovdy caught it.

No goal.

No cheering.

"Too bad, Mia," Garrett said. "Better luck next time."

Mia felt tears in her eyes.

"She's going to quit," whispered Lovdy. "I *knew* it."

Mia still hated losing. But she didn't hate losing as much as she loved soccer.

"Ready to play?" asked Garrett.

Mia nodded.

Garrett grinned at her. He passed her the ball.

Mia ran down the field. Tap, tap, tap with her toes. The ball stayed right with her, like a friend. She got ready to kick it into the goal.

Mia kicked the ball as
hard as she could.

Maybe she'd score
the goal. Maybe
she wouldn't.

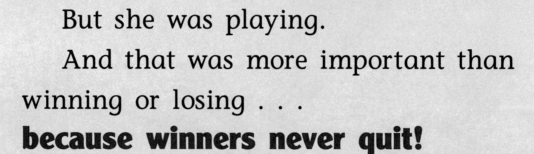

But she was playing.

And that was more important than
winning or losing . . .
because winners never quit!

Your Turn

What Winners Do

Write Directions Write directions that tell how to be a good sport. Tell how to act when you play a game. Tell how to act when you win and when you lose.

SOCIAL STUDIES

Turn and Talk — Mia the Winner

Tell a partner what Mia is like at the beginning of the story. Have your partner tell what she is like at the end. Talk about how she changed.

UNDERSTANDING CHARACTERS

Connect to Social Studies

WORDS TO KNOW

loved	sorry
everyone	only
brothers	people
field	most

GENRE

Informational text gives facts about a topic. Find facts about being on a team in this social studies text.

TEXT FOCUS

A **checklist** is a list of names or things to think about or do. What do you learn from p. 160?

Be a Team Player

Have you ever loved playing on a team? Most people have lots of fun on a team.

All kinds of people play on teams. Sisters and brothers play. Friends and cousins play.

There are all kinds of teams. Some people play baseball or basketball. Some play soccer or volleyball. People may play on a field or on a court.

No matter what kind of team it is, it's important to be a good team player. Try not to feel sorry if you lose a game. Everyone loses sometimes. It's only important to try your best and have fun.

Here is a checklist of things to remember when you play on a team.

Be a Team Player.
✔ Pay attention to the coach.
✔ Follow the rules.
✔ Do your best.
✔ Don't quit.
✔ Have fun!

Making Connections

Text to Self

Write a Poem Write a poem about a time when you were part of a team. Use words that tell about sights, sounds, and feelings.

Text to Text

Talk About It Did Mia become a good team player? Tell why you think so.

Text to World

Connect to Social Studies Name a time when you need to be a team player. Draw a picture to show your idea.

Grammar

Read Together

Adjectives That Compare Add **er** to adjectives to compare two. Add **est** to compare more than two.

Compare Two

Meg is **tall<u>er</u>** than Jon.

Compare More Than Two

Abe is the **tall<u>est</u>** goalie of all.

tall   **taller**   **tallest**

Write adjectives from the boxes to finish the sentences. Use another sheet of paper.

small	smaller	smallest

1. We have a very __?__ soccer team.

2. Our team is the __?__ team in town.

3. Brad's team is __?__ than Eva's team.

fast	faster	fastest

4. I am __?__ than Kyla.

5. Rob is the __?__ runner in the game.

Grammar in Writing

When you revise your writing, try adding some adjectives that compare.

Write to Respond

Read Together

☑ Organization In a good **opinion paragraph**, a topic sentence tells an opinion. A closing sentence retells the opinion in new words.

Tara drafted her paragraph. Then she added a closing sentence.

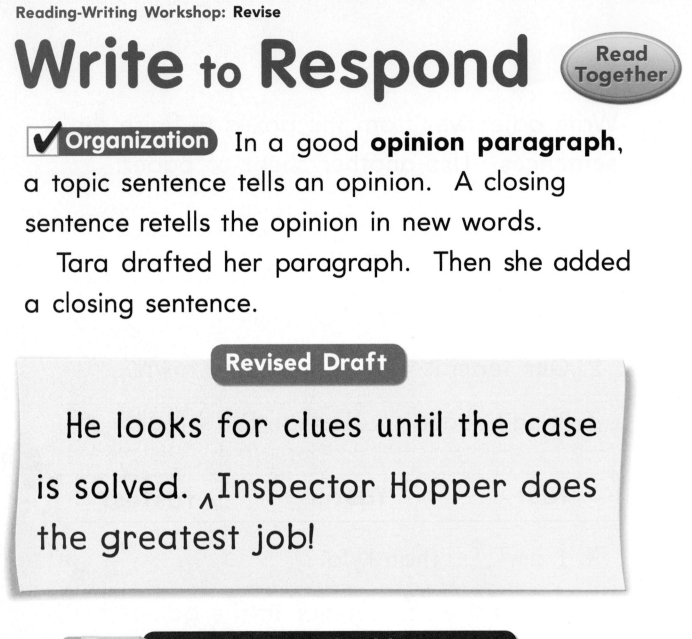

Revised Draft

He looks for clues until the case is solved. ∧Inspector Hopper does the greatest job!

Revise Checklist

☑ Does my topic sentence tell my opinion?

☑ Did I give good reasons for my opinion?

☑ Do I need to add more examples to explain my reasons?

☑ Does my closing sentence retell my opinion?

Which sentence tells Tara's opinion? Which sentence tells it again? Now make changes to revise your draft. Use the Checklist.

Final Copy

Not a Quitter

Inspector Hopper is a very good detective. One reason is because he gets the facts. He finds out what the boat looks like. Also, he doesn't quit. He looks for clues until the case is solved. Inspector Hopper does the greatest job!

Read the next two selections. Then tell how they are alike and different.

A Good Idea

Kit was in the school play. She was happy about it. Kit was also a little scared. She studied her lines, but she did not know a lot of them.

She did not want to give up. Kit asked her brother Jay for help. Jay thought about Kit's lines. He said, "I know that learning a rhyme helps me remember things."

Kit and her brother worked together. They made up some rhymes. Soon Kit knew her lines well. Then she felt good about the play.

"You are the best, Jay!" said Kit. "You have been so helpful."

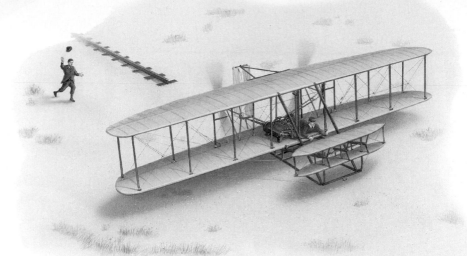

The First Ride

A long time ago, two brothers named Wilbur and Orville Wright built a plane. It was made of wood. The wings were made with cloth. One brother rode on a wing. He had his hands on the controls. The other brother ran next to the plane. He held on to help keep it steady.

The plane went up. It flew for twelve seconds. This may not seem like a long time now, but it was a great time back then!

After this first flight, the brothers made more planes. They learned how to make them better. The Wright brothers helped people learn how to make and fly planes.

Unit 6 Wrap-Up

The Big  Idea

An Award Winner Who do you know who does nice things for others? Who is a good friend? Make an award. Write why you think that person is a winner.

Juan a Friend to All

Listening and Speaking

Guess My Best! Think of something that you do well. Act it out in front of your classmates. The person who guesses what you do well goes next!

Words to Know

Unit 6   High-Frequency Words

㉖ The Dot

teacher	bear
studied	above
surprised	even
toward	pushed

㉙ "A Boat Disappears"

leaves	hello
any	behind
happened	idea
gone	almost

㉗ What Can You Do?

different	high
near	always
enough	once
stories	happy

㉚ Winners Never Quit!

loved	sorry
everyone	only
brothers	people
field	most

㉘ "The Kite"

second	heard
ball	large
across	cried
head	should

Glossary

A

already

Already means before this. My brother was **already** at school by the time my bus arrived.

anyway

Anyway means that something doesn't matter. Mia had a sore foot, but she went to school **anyway**.

B

binoculars

Binoculars are something you look through to make things look closer. Seth looked through the **binoculars** and saw an eagle in a tree.

blank

Blank means with no writing on it. The sheet of paper was **blank**.

C

captain

A **captain** is a kind of leader. Suzie is the **captain** of our swim team.

computers

A **computer** is a machine that works with words, pictures, and numbers. We have two **computers** in our classroom.

D

disappeared

To **disappear** means to stop being seen. The sun **disappeared** behind a cloud.

dribbled

To **dribble** means to use your hands or feet to move a ball from one place to another. Brian **dribbled** the ball past the other players.

F

float

To **float** means to move on top of water. I like to **float** on a raft in the pool.

G

gazing

To **gaze** means to look at something. When Ms. Tam found Ben, he was **gazing** out the window.

goalie

A **goalie** is the player who tries to keep the other team from scoring points. Lupe is the best **goalie** on our soccer team.

H

helpful

To be **helpful** means to help someone do something. I like to be **helpful** by setting the table for dinner.

I

inspector

An **inspector** is someone who looks at things very carefully to try to solve a mystery. The **inspector** asked the woman questions about her lost bag.

J

junk

Junk is something that people do not want. Max and his mom took the **junk** out with the rest of the trash.

L

laughter

Laughter is what you hear when people think something is funny. The story was so funny that we all burst into **laughter.**

N

noticed
To **notice** is to see or hear something. Jason **noticed** the spot on his shirt.

P

perhaps
Perhaps means maybe. **Perhaps** our class will go there on a field trip.

R

rather
Rather is used when you like one thing more than another. I would **rather** ride a bike than walk.

S

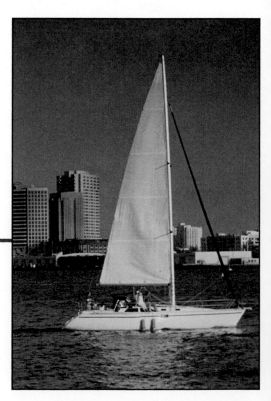

sailed
To **sail** means to move on water in a boat. We quickly **sailed** past the other boats.

solved

To **solve** means to find the answer to a problem. Our class **solved** the problem together.

something

Something means any thing. I wanted to wear **something** red that day.

squiggle

A **squiggle** is a wavy line. My little brother made a **squiggle** with the red crayon.

straight

If something is **straight**, it has no turns or curves. I used a ruler to make my lines **straight**.

swirly

Swirly means in a curving way. Lily used a brush to make **swirly** blue lines on her painting.

Y

yummy

If something is **yummy**, that means it tastes good. That strawberry is **yummy!**

Acknowledgments

"A Boat Disappears" from *Inspector Hopper* by Doug Cushman. Copyright © **2000** by Doug Cushman. All rights reserved. Reprinted by permission of HarperCollins Children's Books, a division of HarperCollins Publishers.

"Caracol, caracol/To a Snail" from *¡Pío Peep!: Traditional Spanish Nursery Rhymes*, selected by Alma Flor Ada & F. Isabel Campoy. Spanish compilation copyright © **2003** by Alma Flor Ada & Isabel Campoy. English adaptation copyright © **2003** by Alice Schertle. Reprinted by permission of HarperCollins Publishers.

Days with Frog and Toad by Arnold Lobel. Copyright © **1979** by Arnold Lobel. All rights reserved. Reprinted by permission of HarperCollins Children's Books, a division of HarperCollins Publishers.

The Dot by Peter H. Reynolds. Copyright © **2003** by Peter H. Reynolds. Reprinted by permission of the publisher Candlewick Press Inc. and Pippin Properties, Inc.

"Song of the Bugs" from *Nibble, Nibble* by Margaret Wise Brown. Copyright © **1959** by William R. Scott, Inc., renewed **1987** by Roberta Brown Rauch. Reprinted by permission of HarperCollins Publishers.

What Can You Do? by Shelley Rotner and Sheila Kelley, with photographs by Shelley Rotner. Coauthor of text and photographs copyright © **2001** by Shelley Rotner. Coauthor of text copyright © **2001** by Sheila Kelley. Reprinted by the permission of Millbrook Press, a division of Lerner Publishing Group. Inc. All rights reserved.

Winners Never Quit! by Mia Hamm, illustrated by Carol Thompson. Text and illustrations copyright © **2004** by Mia Hamm and Byron Preiss Visual Publications, Inc. All rights reserved. Reprinted by permission of HarperCollins Children's Books, a division of HarperCollins Publishers.

"Worm" from *A Little Book of Little Beasts* by Mary Ann Hoberman. Copyright © **1973,** renewed 2001 by Mary Ann Hoberman. Reprinted by permission of Gina Maccoby Literary Agency.

Credits

Photo Credits

Placement Key: (t) top; (b) bottom; (l) left; (r) right; (c) center; (bg) background; (fg) foreground; (i) inset.

8a (c)Blend Images/Tips; **8b** spread (c) BlendImages/Tips Images; **8b** (c)1996 Steve Cole/PhotoDisc; **10** (t) (c)Andreanna Seymore/Stone/Getty Images; **10** (b) (c)Simon Marcus/Corbis; **11** (bl) (c)HMCo.; **11** (br) (c)Howard Grey/Digital Vision/Getty Images; **11** (cl) (c)Bettmann/CORBIS; **11** (tl) (c)Darrin Klimek/Digital Vision/Getty Images; **11** (cr) (c)Mia Foster/PhotoEdit; **11** (tr) (c)Gary Booth; **11** (bl) (c)D. Hurst/Alamy; **13** (c)HMCo.; **14** (c)Courtesy Pippin Properties, Inc. Photo by Dawn Haley Morton; **34** (t) (c)Ellen B. Senisi/The Image Works; **34** (b) (c)Ariel Skelley/Riser/Getty Images; **35** (tl) (c)Cindy Charles/PhotoEdit; **35** (tr) (c)Tony Anderson/Taxi/Getty Images; **35** (cl) (c)Cassy Cohen/PhotoEdit; **35** (cr) (c)Julie Habel/CORBIS; **35** (bl) (c)Corbis; **35** (br) (c)Ariel Skelley/Blend Images/Getty Images; **37** (c) Bill Losh/Taxi/Getty Images; **38** (inset) (c)HMCo.; **39-57** Shelley Rotner; **61** (r) (c)ImageClub; **61** (t) (c)Artville; **61** (b) (c)Stockbyte; **62** (c)Ken Chernus/Taxi/Getty Images; **63** (c)Janine Wiedel Photolibrary/Alamy; **113** (c) Elyse Lewin/The Image Bank/Getty Images; **114** (inset) (c)AFP/Getty Images; **131** (c)Rubberball Productions; **136** (b) (c)Bloomimage/Corbis; **136** (t) (c)1996 Steve Cole/PhotoDisc; **138** (c)C Squared Studios/Getty Images; **139** (c) PhotoDisc/Getty Images; **140** (c) Digital Vision; **141** (c) Eyewire Collection/Getty Images; **142** (c) Digital Stock; **143** (c) Houghton Mifflin Company/School Divison

Illustration

Cover D.B. Johnson; **12** Nathan Jarvis; **41** Chris Lensch; **44** Nathan Jarvis; **66–69** Sam Ward; **73** Jan Bryan-Hunt; **98** Bernard Adnet; **101** Chris Lensch; **128** Bernard Adnet; **126–128** Russel Benfanti; **129** (inset) Ken Bowser; **130–131** Bernard Adnet; **133** Jim Kelly; **163** Bernard Adnet; **165** Sally Vitsky.

All other photos Houghton Mifflin Harcourt Photo Libraries and Photographers.